AMERICAN FOLK ART MUSEUM

Critters a to z

TO

IN AMERICAN FOLK ART

Endpapers:
Butterflies, late 20th century, Maurice Sullins, Joliet, Illinois,
acrylic on canvas, 35 ¾ x 48 in., Blanchard-Hill Collection,
gift of M. Anne Hill and Edward V. Blanchard Jr., 1998.10.52

Opposite:
Eagle and Shield Weathervane, c.1800, artist unidentified,
Massachusetts, cast bell metal, 36 x 43 ½ x 4 in.,
gift of Mr. and Mrs. Francis S. Andrews, 1982.6.4

Front cover credits, see pp. 9, 75. Back cover credit, see p. 17.

Donated and produced by the BIL Charitable Trust
315 East 65th Street, New York, NY 10021

Project Manager/Editor: Barbara Lovenheim
Design: Susan Huyser
Text: Roslyn Siegel

Library of Congress Control Number: 2003101084
ISBN: 0-912161-19-1

Printed by C&C Offset Printing Co., Ltd., Hong Kong

Die erste Welt ließ gott mit Wasser untergehen, Und Noah gieng selb acht in einen kasten ein, Zuletzt wird nun die Welt in lauter Feuer
stehen, Wo wird Zur selben Zeit der Frommen Zuflucht seyn, Ich will, Herr Jesu, mir aus Deiner offnen seiten,
Wenn alles wird vergehn, Ein Arche Zubereiten.

The BIL Charitable Trust, a private foundation dedicated to developing educational materials for non-profit organizations and charities, is pleased to have created this book for the American Folk Art Museum. We believe that it will heighten children's awareness of the diversity of American culture and our common heritage as well as introduce them to the many forms of expression available to artists. I wish to thank Susan Huyser and Roslyn Siegel, both of whom used their talents to make this material accessible and interesting to children, and to Tanya Heinrich, the museum's book editor, who diligently partnered with us to make this book a reality.

Barbara Lovenheim
President, BIL Charitable Trust

Noah's Ark, *c. 1830*
John Landis
Possibly Lancaster County, Pennsylvania
Watercolor and ink on paper, 10 x 13⅝ in.
Promised gift of Ralph Esmerian, P1.2001.241

the critters

All the critters in this book live together at the American Folk Art Museum in New York City. Some of them are almost always out and around, so when you visit the museum you can be sure you'll see them. A six-foot-long tiger will greet you from a ledge as you walk up the stairs—but don't worry; he is friendly. Near the museum café is a group of colorful fish—swimming?—in a small "tank." There is even a smiling dinosaur, but I won't tell you where it is: See if you can find it when you visit. Other critters are shy—they only come out from time to time—but you can read about them in the pages of this book.

American Folk Art Museum critters are made of wood, paper, clay, metal, and other materials—they don't actually run or swim or jump or fly. They live only in the imagination of the artists who created them and the visitors who come and see them. We call these wonderful objects "folk art" because the people who made them learned their skills from other people in their families or in the community in which they lived or because the artists taught themselves how to draw or carve or paint. Many folk artists tell stories through their artwork that help us to better understand the objects they create. Their stories are in this book—A to Z. I invite you to read and enjoy them. And when you are in New York City, please come to the American Folk Art Museum. The critters are here, waiting to greet you.

Gerard C. Wertkin

Director, American Folk Art Museum

Girl in Red Dress with Cat and Dog, *c. 1830–1835*
Ammi Phillips
Vicinity of Amenia, New York
Oil on canvas, 30 x 25 in.
Gift of the Siegman Trust, Ralph Esmerian, trustee,
2001.37.1

a This stylish **armadillo** has a long nose, short, strong legs, and sharp claws to help him dig up the earth and tear apart rotted wood in search of insects and plants to eat. Armadillos are small mammals with armor on their backs made of bony plates that protect them from enemies they might encounter while they are burrowing through the ground. This armadillo also has a flair for fashion, sporting **spots,** stripes, and **triangles** on his strong coat and tail. The figure was carved out of cottonwood by David Alvarez, an artist from Santa Fe, New Mexico. He adapted a **400-year-old** tradition begun by Spanish settlers who carved wooden figures of saints and biblical animals. But this handsome armadillo is not old-fashioned; he looks very much at home in the New World.

(*What other animals eat insects?*)

Armadillo, *c.1984*
David Alvarez
Santa Fe, New Mexico
Housepaint on cottonwood, 7¾ x 5¾ x 18½ in.
Gift of Elizabeth Wecter, 1985.20.1

Lady Holds the Bird, *1991*
Thornton Dial Sr.
Bessemer, Alabama
Watercolor on paper, 22 ¼ x 30 in.
Gift of Ron and June Shelp, 1992.19.3

b Birds, birds, **birds**! Artists the world over have captured the colors, shapes, and free spirits of our feathered friends. In the painting on the left, notice how the curved shape of the blue bird encircles the woman, holding them tightly together. Now they are peaceful and at rest, but at any moment the woman might fly away with the bird, free to soar and find her dreams. Why do you think the artist painted only the head and hands of the woman?

When birds are not flying, they find a spot where they can perch. The bird below is sitting on the edge of an iron **"pie crimper,"** a kitchen tool used to make a ruffled edge on dough used for pie crust. This crimper was made about 200 years ago in Pennsylvania. The jagged **"crimping"** wheel in the middle of the tool pinched and sealed the edge of the crust. The bird's beak was used to cut patterns in the dough.

(What *animal* does the *handle* remind you of?)

Pie Crimper, *c. 1790–1820*
Artist unidentified
Probably southeastern Pennsylvania
Iron, 2⅜ x 8 x ¼ in.
Promised gift of Ralph Esmerian, P1.2001.163

Man Feeding a Bear an Ear of Corn, *c. 1840*
Artist unidentified
Probably Pennsylvania
Watercolor, ink, and pencil on paper, 5 ⅝ x 7 ½ in.
Promised gift of Ralph Esmerian, P1.2001.252

If you were to carve an animal out of a **tree,** *what would it be?*

This **bear** won't tear into the crops of settlers anymore; he's been tamed and trained. See how eagerly he reaches out—his chain taut and his paw extended—as a man in a top hat offers him the ear of corn that he has grown? Even the man in the moon and the cat on the roof seem to watch the scene with approval. Notice how the artist has used the same orange color to paint the house, the stars in the sky, and the flower on the tree. What other colors do you see repeated in the picture?

When wild **buffalo** roamed freely on the great Western plains, they became symbols of power in American history. The buffalo here was carved out of a cedar tree. The rough natural bumps and lumps in a log reminded the artist, Raymond Coins, of the raw power and ◄◄ **LARGE SIZE** ►► of a buffalo. He used branches to make the legs of the buffalo and a big knot on the trunk to form the hump. Using only a simple log, the artist captured the wild, natural spirit of the animal.

Buffalo, *c.1978*
Raymond Coins
Westfield, North Carolina
Cedar, 37 ½ x 49 x 70 in.
Gift of the Gitter-Yelen Collection, 2000.26.1

Cow Jump over the Mone, *1978*
Nellie Mae Rowe
Vinings, Georgia
Colored pencil, crayon, and pencil on paper, 19 ½ x 25 ¼ in.
Gift of Judith Alexander, 1997.10.1

C Wow! What a **COW!** You will probably never see a cow with a woman's face or a moon the color of this one in your world. Nellie Mae Rowe, an African American artist from Georgia, found these ideas in her imagination. She used colored pencils and crayons to express how much she wants to hold up her head and jump over the moon.

The **centaur** below is another imaginative creature you will never see in nature. According to ancient Greek mythology, a centaur has the head of a man and the body of a horse, making him very wise and also very strong. These qualities make him perfect for a **" weathervane, "** since he can stand up in the wind and **alert farmers to changes in the weather.** This centaur is made of copper and covered in gold leaf, a very thin sheet of gold. It stood on top of a barn in New Hampshire about 150 years ago.

(If you could be half-animal, what animal would it be?)

Centaur Weathervane, *1852–1867*
Probably A.L. Jewell & Company
Waltham, Massachusetts
Copper with gold leaf, with iron directionals, 50½ x 43 x 29 in.
Promised gift of Ralph Esmerian, P1.2001.327

Be careful! If this tabby **cat** falls down, he won't land on his feet. This cat can break very easily since he is molded of plaster of Paris, a fragile material that looks like chalk. Figures like this were called **"chalkware."** They were made primarily by Italian immigrants who lived in large cities like Boston, New York, and Philadelphia in the early 1900s. Since house cats were popular pets, many Americans bought these chalk cats to decorate their homes.

Meow! You can almost feel the fur on the **mother cat and kittens** ✳ here. They seem to look at you with as much interest as you look at them. The artist, Morris Hirshfield, gave each kitten different markings and a different curve in the tail, so that each cat has a different personality. Notice how carefully the artist painted the ● ● ● **dots** ● ● ● on the carpet and how he used his brush to make lines on the floor. He also made a decorative border to hold the family together.

✳ *What would you name each kitten?* ▶

Seated Cat, *1850–1900*
Artist unidentified
Eastern United States
Paint on plaster of Paris, 15 ⅝ x 8 ¾ x 10 ⅛ in.
Gift of Effie Thixton Arthur, 1963.3.1

Mother Cat with Kittens, *1941*
Morris Hirshfield
Brooklyn, New York
Oil on canvas, 24 x 36 in.
Gift of Patricia L. and Maurice C. Thompson Jr. and
purchase with funds from the Jean Lipman Fellows, 1998.5.1
©Robert and Gail Rentzer for the Estate of Morris Hirshfield /
Licensed by VAGA, New York

Dragon, *c.1943*
Victor Joseph Gatto
New York City
Oil on canvas, 16 x 19¾ in.
Gift of Ken and Asa Miller, 1985.6.2

(What **features** do
dragons and dinosaurs
have in common?)

ho's the fiercest of them all? The fire-spouting **dragon** in the painting on the left? Or the carved dinosaur below? They look a lot alike. But dragons are imaginary winged reptiles; dinosaurs were real prehistoric reptiles. To create a thick texture on the dragon's scaly back, the artist stripped his brush of all but a few hairs. Then he slowly applied several layers of paint over and over. See how the sharp curve of the dragon's claws is repeated in its teeth and horns to enhance its ferocious appearance?

Fred Alten, the artist who carved this **dinosaur,** made animals in his garage without telling anyone. Using a penknife and simple materials—**wood, paint, and wax**—he created more than 150 animals. Most were painted black, regardless of the creature's natural color. This wooden reptile has the short forelegs, strong hindlegs, and long, curving tail typical of many dinosaurs. But while most dinosaurs were fierce, this guy's bright eyes and big red smile give him a distinctly friendly personality.

Dinosaur, *1915–1925*
Fred Alten
Wyandotte, Michigan
Paint on wood, 9 3/8 x 24 5/8 x 3 1/2 in.
Gift of Mr. and Mrs. Joseph A. Dumas, 1977.2.1

What other animals have good profiles? Try drawing one with just **one** **color** to show its personality.

Dog, *1939–1942*
Bill Traylor
Montgomery, Alabama
Pencil, crayon, and poster paint on cardboard,
18 ¼ x 26 ½ in.
Gift of Herbert Waide Hemphill Jr., 1990.1.1

This is a **dog** with **attitude!** He takes up the whole space on the cardboard with his tongue stuck out, his eye wide open, and his tail alert, ready for anything. His plain brown coat, unpainted paws, and simple, flat profile show that he is **no fancy pooch— and proud of it.** The artist, Bill Traylor, was enslaved and then a freed farmworker in Alabama. When he moved to the city of Montgomery at the age of 84, he also **freed his artistic spirit.** Using materials he found on the street—cardboard, old pencil stubs, crayons, and leftover paint—he painted about 1,500 works in just three years.

The **seated dog** on the right has a more welcoming posture than the dog on the left. Her round **pink eyes** and **red mouth** brighten her bumpy appearance. The artist, Sam Doyle, lived on a rural island off the South Carolina coast. He captured the spirit of the island in his work and used common materials for his paintings and sculptures. This dog was carved from a tree log and covered with tar. Her tongue is made of painted tin.

Seated Dog, *late 20th century*
Sam Doyle
St. Helena Island, South Carolina
Paint on wood with tin and tar, 19 x 23 x 8 in.
Blanchard-Hill Collection, gift of M. Anne Hill and
Edward V. Blanchard Jr., 1998.10.20

On this miniature weathervane, the male **deer** is poised and alert, perhaps ready to protect the doe on the opposite page. Notice how his elegant antlers and the **"symmetry"** (balance) of his legs contribute to his erect posture. He was made about 150 years ago by J. Howard and Company, a small workshop in Massachusetts. J. Howard, the owner and chief artist, was also a farmer. His encounters with the neighboring deer probably helped him capture its watchful spirit so perfectly.

The gentle doe in the **"fraktur"** on the right has nothing to worry about since a crowned angel is watching over her. A fraktur is a handwritten text that was often illustrated with flowers, birds, and figures. Documents of this kind were made by Pennsylvania German artists in the 18th and 19th centuries. Fraktur were used to record important occasions and teach penmanship to students. This "presentation" fraktur was given to a schoolchild as a reward, similar to the **gold stars** that young children are awarded today.

Miniature Deer Weathervane, *c. 1852–1867*
Attributed to J. Howard & Company
West Bridgewater, Massachusetts
Paint on zinc and copper, 12 ¾ x 9 x 5 in.
Promised gift of Ralph Esmerian, P1.2001.334

**Presentation Fraktur
with Angel and Doe,** *1789*
Johann Adam Eyer
*Probably Bedminster Township,
Pennsylvania*
*Watercolor and ink
on paper, 7 ⁷⁄₁₆ x 4 ¾ in.*
*Promised gift of
Ralph Esmerian, P1.2001.203*

You may have an **eagle** in your pocket right now—if you have a quarter. Eagles symbolize the power and strength of the United States and are found often in ★★★American★★★ folk art. They appear on furniture, bedcovers, weathervanes, and paintings and are even carved on the prows of ships. This fierce eagle was made about 1890 by

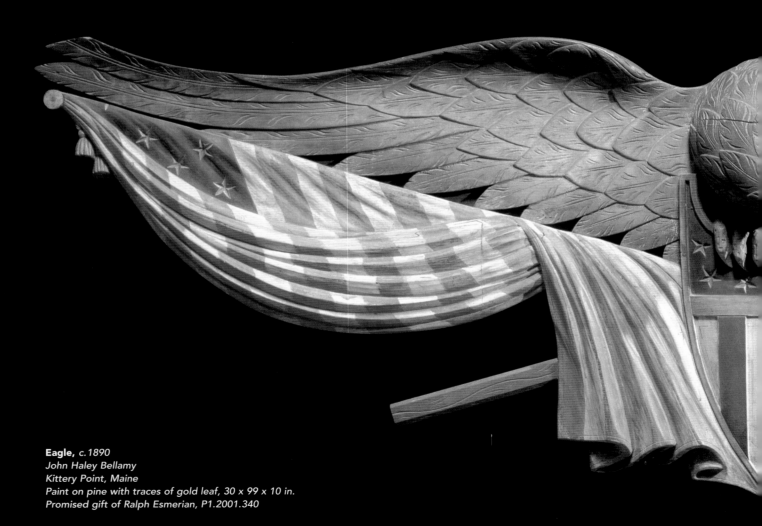

Eagle, *c.1890*
John Haley Bellamy
Kittery Point, Maine
Paint on pine with traces of gold leaf, 30 x 99 x 10 in.
Promised gift of Ralph Esmerian, P1.2001.340

John Haley Bellamy, a woodcarver in Maine. The eagle is perched on top of two draped ★ ★ ★American★ ★ ★ flags, guarding them with his sharp, hooked beak, his long claws, and his deeply carved wings more than ◀◀ **8 FEET LONG.**▶▶ He has a keen "eagle eye" and is ready to fly off to protect freedom and democracy. It's likely he was carved for a public building, where he could carefully watch over the townspeople.

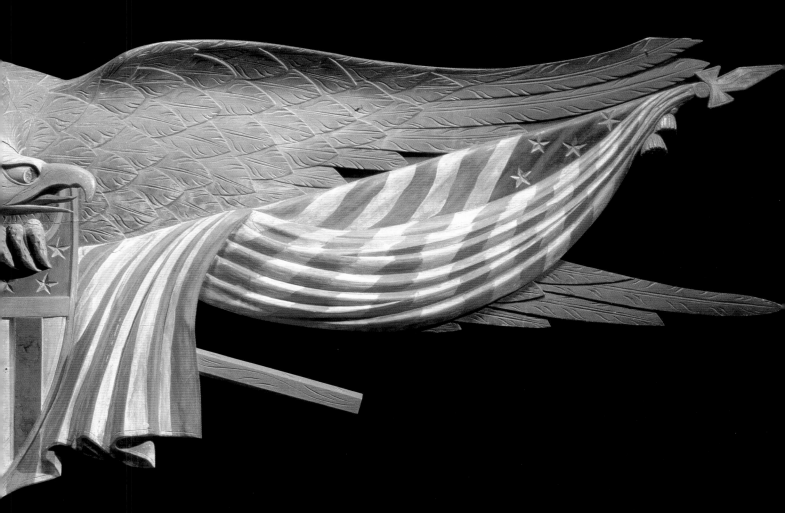

What an encounter with an **elephant!** The artist, John Podhorsky, created a whole fantasy landscape teeming with activity and color. Horses and elephants live side by side. Houses in different styles stand in the same neighborhood. There is frantic movement in all directions as a rowboat collides with a building and a woman in a polka-dot dress rides her horse straight into the elephant! Clusters of letters don't always make real words and, although the artist named this picture *Houses and Two Hundred Animals,* there are not nearly that many animals here. This is a **strange, dreamlike world,** but we can still appreciate the **wonderful energy and color of all the images, falling over each other fighting for space.**

Every inch of this paper is covered with squiggles, scribbles, and figures to enjoy. Here is a universe of dancing color and line!

Houses and Two Hundred Animals, *c.1950s*
John Podhorsky
Auburn, California
Pencil, colored pencil, and crayon on paper, 24 x 35 ½ in.
Blanchard-Hill Collection, gift of M. Anne Hill
and Edward V. Blanchard Jr., 1998.10.37

Fish Flask or Bottle, *c. 1800–1822*
Attributed to Rudolph Christ
Salem, North Carolina
Glazed red earthenware, 2⅝ x 4½ x 1⅜ in.
Promised gift of Ralph Esmerian, P1.2001.153

f There's something fishy going on here! The mouth of the large green **fish** on the left is really the opening of a bottle. It was made around 200 years ago in North Carolina, in an area rich in fine clay. The vessel was formed by pressing soft clay into a plaster mold. When the clay hardened, it was removed from the mold and painted with a chemical glaze. After it was fired in a pottery furnace called a **"kiln,"** the glaze turned a shiny, luminous green. Have you ever seen a green fish?

The fish below look real but they are actually **"decoys"** made of wood and metal and painted with bright colors to look like real trout and perch. Ice fishermen walk onto frozen lakes, cut holes in the ice, drop decoys into the water, and wait. When real fish are fooled into swimming toward the decoys, the fishermen drop their hooks or aim their spears. The fish that fall for this trick are cooked—for dinner!

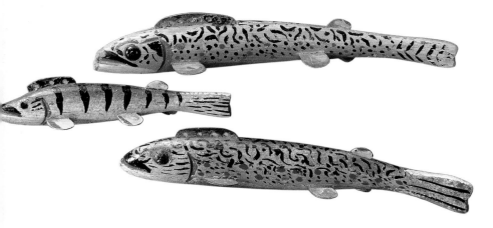

Trout, Perch, and Brook Trout Decoys, *1935–1944*
Oscar "Pelee" Peterson
Cadillac, Michigan
Paint on wood and metal, 5 in. to 7 in. long
Trout decoy, gift of Alan Milton, 1990.14.1;
perch and brook trout decoys, gift of Lori Zabar
in memory of Selma Segal, 1991.14.4,5

(*What other animals might be hiding in the jungle?*)

Jungle Scene, *1942*
Victor Joseph Gatto
Probably New York City
Oil on canvas, 24 x 29½ in.
Gift of Ellin and Baron Gordon in memory
of Herbert Waide Hemphill Jr., 2000.9.1

g In this lush jungle, a gentle **giraffe** is living with an elephant and a herd of tigers. To create this exotic world, the artist swirled layers of thick, wet paint on the canvas, creating a dense, tropical forest filled with twisting branches, spiky leaves, and unusual flowers. The strong outlines of the leaves, the irregular pattern on the giraffe's back, and the crowded canvas—filled all over with strange shapes, layers of color, and wild brush strokes—produce a strong sense of movement and excitement.

This giant **grasshopper** is not a super-insect that has escaped from a science fiction movie but a rare weathervane created around 1880 to sit on the roof of a stable in Massachusetts. Made of copper, the weathervane was coated with a thin covering of **" gold leaf. "** After years of exposure to the sun, wind, rain, and snow, the gold leaf wore off in places, exposing copper that over time developed a **" patina "** — a beautiful coating shaded green.

Grasshopper Weathervane, *c. 1880*
Artist unidentified
Marlboro, Massachusetts
Molded copper with gold leaf, 17 x 35 x 9 in.
Gift of Mr. and Mrs. Francis S. Andrews, 1982.6.6

31

The mythical **griffin** in the middle panel on the right is an imaginary creature that is half-bird and half-lion. This illustration appears in an old puzzle book for children that is similar to today's flip-books. These puzzle books were also called "turn-ups" or **"metamorphosis"** books, because the images merge and **"morph"** as the pages are turned quickly. When the head of the **lion (1)** is flipped up, a **griffin (2)** emerges. When the tail is flipped down, the creature becomes a **bird (3).**

This little fellow is probably a billy **goat** and not a nanny goat because of his beard. He has a mottled (spotted) coat of many colors—brown, orange, red, and tan. He was made about 150 years ago in Virginia. The potter shaped the figure by hand with red clay, then covered the clay with different kinds of **"slip,"** a liquid mixture of clay and chemicals. When the figure was fired in a kiln, the slip melted and the colors ran together, resulting in a shiny, colorful glaze.

Seated Goat, *c.1870–1889*
Anthony Wise Baecher
Winchester, Virginia
Glazed red earthenware, 6 ⅞ x 7 ⅝ x 2 ³⁄₁₆ in.
Promised gift of Ralph Esmerian, P1.2001.151

*What imaginary animal can **you** create out of two other animals in three easy steps?*

1

2

3

Metamorphosis, *1794*
Artist unidentified
Probably New England
Watercolor and ink on paper, 6¹⁄₁₆ x 3³⁄₁₆ in. (folded)
Promised gift of Ralph Esmerian, P1.2001.253c

Prancing Horses, *1937*
Lawrence Lebduska
New York City
Oil on canvas, 16 x 20 in.
Museum purchase, 1984.19.1

h

One of the prancing **horses** in the painting on the left is pink. One is **aqua-blue.** *See what imagination can do!* The soft, dreamy colors here lift the images from the real world into the world of fantasy. The artist, Lawrence Lebduska, grew up in Germany, where he learned the craft of making stained glass. After immigrating to the United States in the early 1900s, he began to paint using many of the same techniques. See how the light comes through the clouds in the lavender and turquoise sky as if through a window?

This family of a rooster, **hens,** and chicks can be moved like pieces in a game from ● one ● peg ● hole ● to ● another ● Leroy Person, the artist who made these unusual feathered friends, applied so many layers of ordinary crayon to the wood that it looks a lot like paint. Deep grooves carved into the figures give the impression of feathers and wings; lines on the base look like marks made by scratching and pecking. With simple gestures and bold colors, he made a lively barnyard scene. *Who is the ruler of the roost?*

Hens and Chicks with Rooster,
mid- to late 20th century
Leroy Person
Occhineechee Neck, North Carolina
Crayon on wood, 13 x 15⅜ x 8½ in.
Gift of Roger Cardinal in memory
of Timothy Grutzius, 1995.14.1

What kinds of **sounds**
do you think these creatures
would make?

Zoo of Tin Can Creatures,
mid- to late 20th century
Artist unidentified
New York City
Paint on tin with plastic jewels, 1 to 4 ½ in. high
Gift of Jack L. Goldstein, 2002.7.1

The unidentified artist who made these tin can creatures — **insects,** by the looks of them — had quite an imagination. With a few snips, twists, and curls, ordinary tin cans were turned into what seem to be beautiful bugs. Then they were brightened with a few dabs of paint and colorful plastic jewels, creating an entire zoo filled with sixty-two creepy-crawlers. Just imagine these zany critters **moving** along the ground and **buzzing** through the air with their **spindly legs, alert antennae, flickering wings,** and **colorful shells.** Which one resembles a spider? A beetle? A mosquito? Or do these critters remind you of other animals in the natural world?

A gentle **jaguar**—or is it a leopard—lying beside a friendly fox? A tame lion and a bear behind him? If these wild animals could live peacefully with children, lambs, and goats, then maybe people of all types can live in harmony as well. Edward Hicks, the artist who painted this picture in the mid-1800s, belonged to the **"Quakers,"** a religious group also known as the Religious Society of Friends. Quakers believe that people should resolve their differences peacefully. Members refuse to fight or go to war. To express these ideals, Hicks decided to illustrate the **peaceable kingdom** described in the Bible—he painted variations of the same scene more than sixty-two times! William Penn, the founder of Pennsylvania, is shown signing a peace treaty with the Indians. A child in the lower left corner is holding a dangerous snake. *Can you find the bald eagle, the national bird of America, guarding this restful kingdom?*

*What **animals** in the picture can you name?*

The Peaceable Kingdom, *c. 1846–1848*
Edward Hicks
Newtown, Pennsylvania
Oil on canvas, 26 x 29 ⅜ in.
Promised gift of Ralph Esmerian, P1.2001.59

Hip-*hop.* Hip-*hop.* Maybe this leaping **kangaroo** can perform gold-medal jumps. But look at the the sharp teeth and the long curving neck. What prehistoric creature does it resemble? The unidentified artist in Pennsylvania who carved this wooden animal in the mid-1900s probably never saw a real kangaroo, since the hopping **" marsupials "** live far away in Australia and New Guinea. So he carved his own imaginative kangaroo, painted it red, and covered it with **● ● ● spots● ● ●** Look at the position of the kangaroo's strong back legs and short forelegs, the curling tail, and the perked-up ears. This kangaroo is ready to bounce!

Kangaroo, *mid-19th century*
Artist unidentified
Probably Pennsylvania
Paint on wood, 28 x 49 ½ x 5 in.
Promised gift of Ralph Esmerian, P1.2001.160

The regal **lion** on the right—with his challenging stare, his dense mane, and his long, lean body—projects power and dignity. His shape is cut from a piece of carpet with lots of closely woven fibers. The bright orange background is painted with flowers and animals and suggests the **fertile African jungle.** The curving black lines add **movement** and **vitality** to the work. The artist, Thornton Dial Jr., an African American, grew up in Alabama, but he often painted the natural beauty and lushness of his people's homeland.

The tranquil **loon** below is a rare **"decoy"** made of wood. Loons are heavier than most other waterbirds—their closest relatives are penguins—since they do a lot of swimming and diving, rather than flying. Loons are inedible and were not hunted as much as ducks and geese. Therefore, loon decoys are **scarce and hard to find.** This graceful loon with its long neck and slender beak was probably made in the early 20th century in New England.

Loon Decoy, *early 20th century*
Artist unidentified
Probably New England
Paint on wood, 19 x 12 x 3 ½ in.
Bequest of Winifred P. Eichler,
1992.21.1

King of Africa, *1989*
Thornton Dial Jr.
Bessemer, Alabama
Enamel on carpet and incised wood with
industrial sealing compound, 48 x 72 in.
Museum purchase made possible with grants
from the National Endowment for the Arts
and the Metropolitan Life Foundation, 1990.3.2

(*What other animals have scales on their tails?*)

**Presentation Fraktur of Merfolk, Flowers,
and Crown,** *c.1785*
Johann Henrich Otto
Probably Lancaster or Lebanon County, Pennsylvania
Watercolor and ink on block-printed paper, 6 ⅜ x 8 ¹⁄₁₆ in.
Promised gift of Ralph Esmerian, P1.2001.195

m

This image of a **mermaid** (half-woman, half-fish) and merman (half-man, half-fish) was created around 1785 using a **"woodcut."** The picture was first carved on a flat panel of wood, coated in black ink, and then pressed onto paper to reproduce the image. When the ink dried, the woodcut was filled in with bright watercolors. This process is similar to rubber stamps or potato stamps.

This little **mouse** is too busy thinking about his own dinner to worry about the cat ready to pounce on him. These playful figures were made by Alex Sandoval, a miner in New Mexico. He began carving figures from aspen, pine, and cottonwood when he was 79 years old, using **ordinary household materials** to complete them. Here the mouse's tail is made of a plastic drinking straw, and the cat's tail is made of telephone wire. Because Sandoval was colorblind, his wife painted yellow eyes, pink paws, and ■ ■ **rectangular** ■ **sp**■**ts** ■ ■ to give these critters a more realistic appearance.

Cat and Mouse on a Board, *c. 1985*
Alejandro "Alex" Sandoval
Santa Fe, New Mexico
Paint on cottonwood with plastic straw, telephone wire,
and staples mounted on wood board, 5 ½ x 5 x 23 ¾ in.
Gift of Elizabeth Wecter, 1985.20.35

n

Who? Whooo? Whoooo is waking up this **night owl?** It certainly looks startled with its eyes wide open and ears perked up. Owls are " **nocturnal** " birds—they sleep during the day and fly around at night to hunt for food. An unidentified artist in Pennsylvania painted this watercolor in the early 1800s. Since it was difficult to spot owls during the day, the artist must have gotten a good look at a real owl at night. Notice how carefully he used a brush to make dabs of colored feathers and to highlight the owl's sharp beak—good for eating insects and little mice—and sharp ears—good for hearing creatures in the night.

(*What other animals sleep* *during the day?*)

Presentation Fraktur of an Owl, *c. 1810*
Artist unidentified
Probably Lehigh County, Pennsylvania
Watercolor and ink on paper, 5 ¼ x 3 ½ in.
Promised gift of Ralph Esmerian, P1.2001.223

47

The confident **ostriches** at the center of the quilt on the left are standing at attention—they're not hiding their heads in the sand, as many ostriches do. The quiltmaker cut animals, flowers, fruit, and figures out of newspaper and traced the patterns onto shiny fabric called "chintz." The fabric shapes were cut and sewn onto a large bedspread to make a colorful quilt with many different animals and designs. The process is called "**appliqué**" because shapes from one fabric are applied or sewn onto another fabric. Almost all the animals and birds are in pairs. What other pairs do you see?

With no jungle or zoo, what's an **orangutan** to do? This one is preparing to swing from tree to tree, with his long arms upraised and his knees bent at sharp angles. The artist in New Mexico who made this hairy ape gave the monkey's feet, hands, chest, and face a coat of glossy black paint. **Then he glued tangled strands of sisal rope to the rest of his body to create fur.**

Bird of Paradise Quilt Top, *1858–1863*
Artist unidentified
Vicinity of Albany, New York
Cotton, wool, silk, and ink
with silk embroidery, 84 ½ x 69 ⅝ in.
Gift of the Trustees, 1979.7.1

Seated Orangutan, *c. 1978*
Alonzo Jimenez
Chupadero, New Mexico
Paint on cottonwood with sisal twine, 62 x 51 x 34 in.
Gift of Elizabeth Wecter, 1985.20.22

p This pleasant **pheasant** weathervane was carved around 1875 in Connecticut. The hen's long, sweeping tail feathers, or **"plumage,"** was designed to shift in the wind to alert farmers to changes in the weather. The artist gave the pheasant strong wings typical of eagles. See how carefully each feather was carved, transforming the hard wood into soft, flowing curves? Perched on the roof of a barn, this pheasant would be beautiful to watch, even in a storm.

Prickle, prickle, quills don't tickle on this perky **porcupine!** David Alvarez, an artist who lives in New Mexico, used straw to make this critter's quills. Maybe these fake quills won't sting your skin, but they will scratch and bristle. So even though this critter looks cute, he's not the cuddly type. **Keep your distance!**

Porcupine, *c.1981*
David Alvarez
Santa Fe, New Mexico
Paint on cottonwood with straw,
marbles, and plastic, 19 x 13 x 35 in.
Gift of Elizabeth Wecter, 1985.20.4

(What other birds have **long tails?**)

Pheasant Hen Weathervane, *c. 1875*
Artist unidentified
Probably Connecticut
Pine with traces of paint, 22 x 31 x 10 in.
Promised gift of Ralph Esmerian, P1.2001.333

The woman in this drawing is pretty as the **peacock** below in her splendid dress, which echoes the brilliant colors, shapes, and ruffled feathers of nature's showy bird. The artist, Consuelo "Chelo" González Amézcua, used **"motifs"** (designs) from her native Mexico. The scalloped edge of the dress looks like Mexican lacework; other patterns imitate traditional Mexican **embroidery** and paper cutouts. In one hand the woman holds a **"gourd"** (a hollow rind used to hold liquid) spilling water **droplets.** In the other hand, she holds a vibrant, patterned shawl. Using an ordinary ballpoint pen, the artist produced a drawing that **dances** with color and movement.

In the World, *1962*
Consuelo "Chelo" González Amézcua
Del Rio, Texas
Ballpoint pen on paper, 28 x 22 in.
Blanchard-Hill Collection, gift of
M. Anne Hill and Edward V. Blanchard Jr.,
1998.10.1

THE RESIDENCE OF DAVID TWINING.1785.

The Residence of David Twining 1785, *1846*
Edward Hicks
Newtown, Pennsylvania
Oil on canvas, in original wood frame with paint
and gold leaf, 30 ½ x 35 ⅞ x 1 ⅜ in. (framed)
Promised gift of Ralph Esmerian, P1.2001.60

Pig Bottle or Flask, *c. 1830–1860*
Attributed to Daniel Henne or Joseph Henne
Shartlesville, Pennsylvania
Glazed red earthenware, 4 ⅝ x 11 x 4 ⅛ in.
Promised gift of Ralph Esmerian,
P1.2001.135

This pudgy **pig** is really a "**flask**" (bottle) made of clay about 150 years ago. The potter pressed moist clay into two matching sides of a mold and joined the sides with liquid clay called "**slip.**" Then he added the tail, ears, and legs and made the snout into a drinking spout. He scratched ridges onto the pig's body to give it a bristly, piggy surface, dipped it into a glaze to make it waterproof, and fired it in a kiln.

There's an **entire family of pigs** in the painting on the left, lined up neatly according to size. The artist, Edward Hicks, grew up on the Twining farm in Pennsylvania. When he was 61, he painted this scene from happy memories of his youth. The Twinings were **Quakers,** and Hicks drew himself standing at the knee of Elizabeth Twining, who is reading to him. Other members of the family are also pictured. Before cameras were invented, paintings like these served as **important records of people and places.**

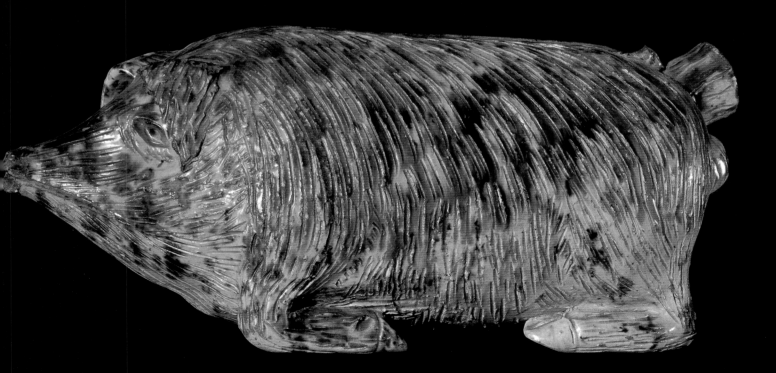

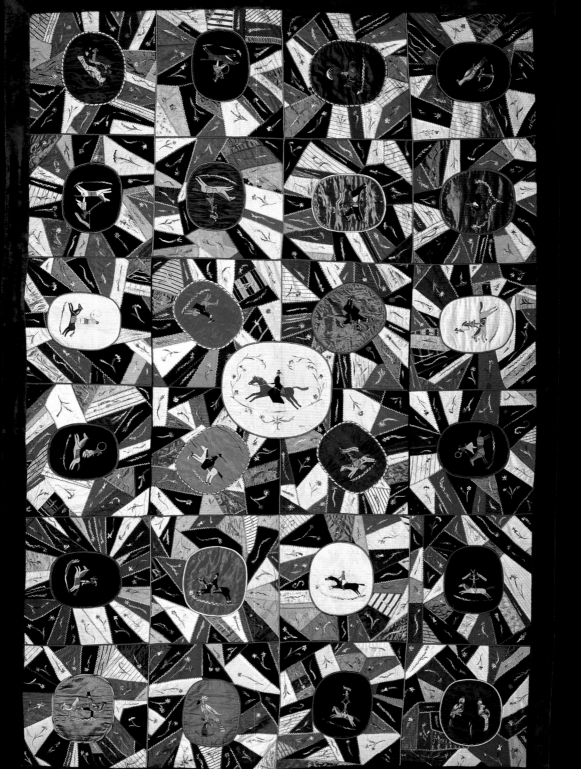

Clip-clop. Clip-clop. The spirited **quarter horse** below may be prancing off the plate to join the horses sewn onto the quilt on the left. Quarter horses were first bred in 17th-century America to race on **"quarter mile"** tracks. The bugle and sword indicate that the rider on this plate—made in 1805 by John Neis, a potter in Pennsylvania—was probably a member of the United States cavalry (a soldier on horseback).

There are **20 quarter horses** in this crazy quilt, which was made in the late 1800s. Unlike quilts made up of regularly shaped patches of colorful material sewn together to create a repeated pattern, **"crazy quilts"** are composed of irregular shapes without a pattern. But this quilt is a "contained" crazy, because the shapes are contained within uniform squares.

Equestrian Crazy Quilt, *1880–1900*
Artist unidentified
Possibly New York State
Silk, velvet, and cotton
with cotton embroidery, 92 x 61 ½ in.
Gift of Mr. and Mrs. James D. Clokey III, 1986.12.1

Sgraffito Plate
with Horse and Rider, *1805*
John Neis
Upper Salford Township, Pennsylvania
Glazed red earthenware, 12 ⅜ in. diam.
Promised gift of Ralph Esmerian, P1.2001.132

r Why is this roly-poly **ram** with a big belly and colorful horns staring right at you? Using simple round shapes that are repeated in the ram's eyes, belly, and body, the artist created an imposing animal. As inspiration, the artist, William Hawkins, used a photograph of a male sheep in a magazine. Why do you think he painted his ram **red, white, and blue?**

This **rabbit** was designed to jump up and down, but she never gets very far. She was made for a **"carousel"** (merry-go-round) in the early 20th century. The woodcarver worked for the Dentzel Company in Philadelphia, the first and largest carousel company in the United States. This rabbit rode on the inside ring of the carousel, possibly amid lions, tigers, giraffes, ostriches, pigs, cats, and even swans!

Carousel Rabbit, c.1915
Dentzel Company
Philadelphia
Paint on wood with glass,
57 ¼ x 49 x 12 ½ in.
Promised gift of Ralph Esmerian,
P1.2001.352

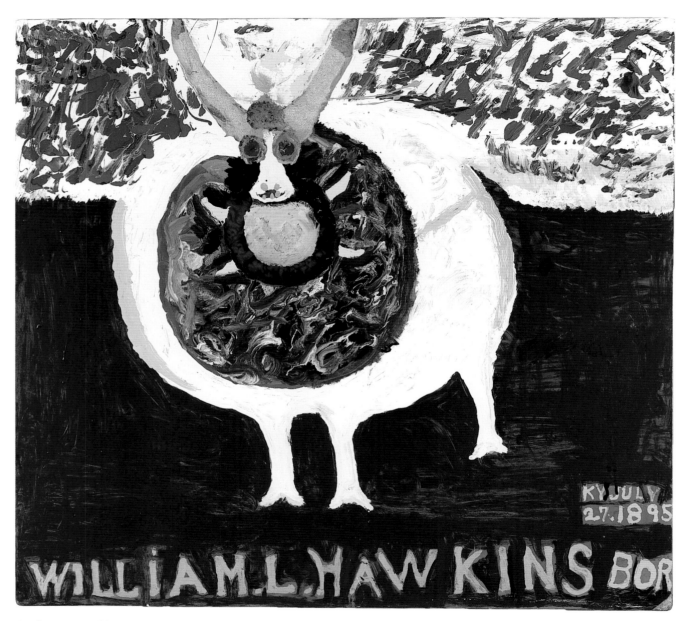

Jacob's Ram, *c. 1986*
William L. Hawkins
Columbus, Ohio
Enamel on Masonite, 36 x 38 ½ in.
Gift of Dan and Jeanne Fauci /
Outside-in Gallery, Los Angeles, 1991.20.1

What other animals have
round bodies?

Windmill with Rooster, *c.1950*
David Butler
Patterson, Louisiana
Paint on tin with wood and plastic,
29 ¼ x 49 ½ x 24 ¼ in.
Gift of William A. Fagaly in honor of
Bruce Johnson, 1977.15.1

Run, **rooster,** *run!* This **whirligig** twirls and rotates in the wind, driven by blades and paddles made of wood and unusual-shaped pieces of tin. It is so filled with exciting colors and shapes that it seems to move even when it's standing still. *Can you find the plastic jack-o'-lantern face on the front?* Or the blue and red speckled rooster with flapping silver wings? The artist, David Butler, worked in sawmills in Louisiana. When he was 62, he began creating extraordinary

sculptures to decorate his window and yard, using tin that he cut with a knife or a chisel and hammer. He embellished his unusual cutouts with **bright paint**, plastic toys, pinwheels, and costume jewelry. Butler also decorated a bicycle adorned with painted tin and pinwheels that he rode through his neighborhood, **delighting children in the area.**

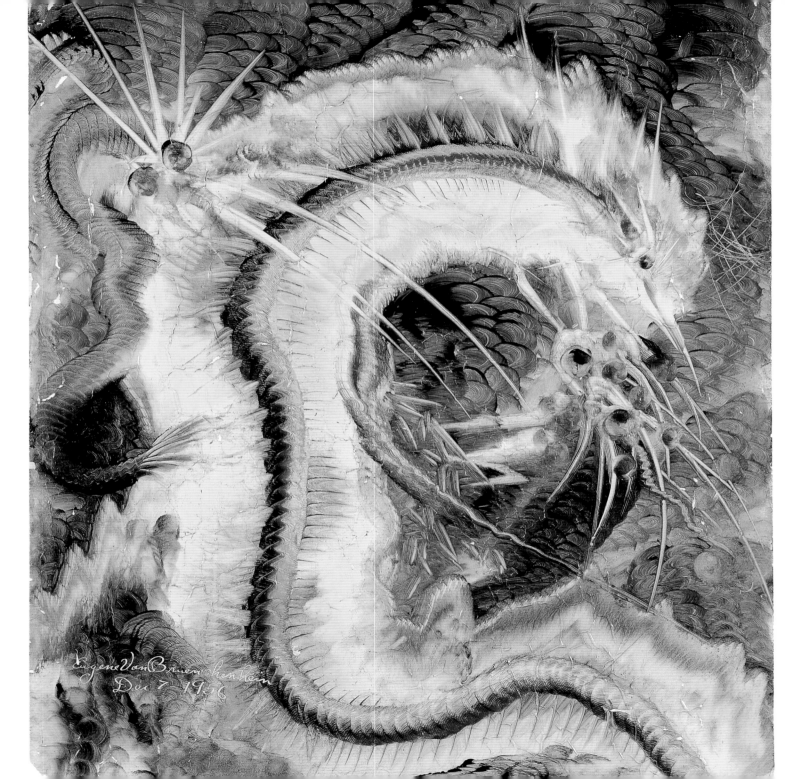

S Ahoy there! The curvy **sea serpent** below is a 19th-century weathervane inspired by the supposed sightings of these imaginary creatures off the coasts of New England. A sea serpent is a "**hybrid**" (combination) animal with the head of a sea horse and the tail of a snake that appears in ancient mythology. As New Englanders in the 1800s became interested in finding new species, many reported that they had seen actual sea serpents in the ocean. *What other imaginary creature does it look like?*

The colorful **serpent** in the painting on the left is even more fantastical. The artist, Eugene Von Bruenchenhein, a former baker, used his fingers to paint and create patterns and texture. Here he re-creates the **fiery explosion of atomic energy.** The serpent's "**luminous**" (light-filled) body hovers over the landscape below. Can you see a resemblance between the shapes in the green background and the serpent's scales? How many serpents can you find in the painting?

Dec. 7-1956 (#211), 1956
Eugene Von Bruenchenhein
Milwaukee, Wisconsin
Oil on Masonite, 17 x 15 in.
Gift of Lewis and Jean Greenblatt,
2000.1.27

Sea Serpent Weathervane, *c. 1850*
Artist unidentified
New England
Paint on wood with iron,
16 ¼ x 23 ¼ x 1 in.
Museum purchase, 1981.12.13

Grotesque Face Jug, *1976*
Lanier Meaders
Mossy Creek, Georgia
Ash-glazed stoneware, 8⅝ x 7⅝ in. diam.
Gift of Mr. and Mrs. Charles Rosenak, 1980.3.12

S-s-see the s-s-spotted **snake** s-s-slithering out of the mouth of this jug shaped like a face? The artist, Lanier Meaders, worked in his family's pottery business in Georgia. He became known for creating powerful **face jugs,** some of them **"grotesque,"** like this one. Meaders used clay from a local creek for the jug's face and white porcelain for the eyes and teeth.

The twisting **snakes** below are **snaking their way up** these old walking sticks. Snakes are often carved onto canes because the shape of a snake's body can be easily wrapped around the shaft of a cane—and snakes were a familiar sight to any walker in the country. How are these three snakes *different?*

(Draw a picture of a snake wound around an object.)

All of these canes were created in the late 19th or early 20th century in the eastern United States, artists unidentified. Left to right:
Snake Cane, paint on poplar and wisteria with glass and cat's teeth, 33 ½ x 2 in. diam.
Snake Cane with Nesting Birds Handle, paint on wood with brads and metal thimble ferrule, 38 ¼ x 2 ¼ in. diam.
Snake Cane with Fist Handle, paint on olive wood with ivory, brads, and brass, 34 ½ x 2 in. diam.
All promised gifts of Ralph Esmerian, P1.2001.362–4

t

This imposing **tiger** may be a good tracker, but she has a friendly smile on her face. And, even though she is licking her chops, she probably won't make a meal of the hard-shelled turtle. The artist, Felipe Archuleta, who lived in New Mexico, carved animals from soft cottonwood. He added features with items such as bits of rubber tires, leather, straw, and marbles. A gigantic brush of straw forms the tiger's whiskers, framing a full set of sharp teeth. Bold stripes decorate her ◀◀ **SIX-FOOT-LONG** ▶▶ body.

Maybe some **turtles** are slow moving, but the turtle here is ready to race a hare—or a **tiger!** Made to be a footstool, this turtle was carved from wood and painted black. White spots on his back add to his **snappy** personality. A curved branch from a tree forms his neck and head.

Tigere, 1977
Felipe Benito Archuleta
Tesuque, New Mexico
Paint and gesso on cottonwood with straw,
32 ½ x 71 x 17 in.
Gift of George H. Meyer, 2000.17.1

Turtle, *19th century*
Artist unidentified
United States
Paint on wood, 7 ¼ x 20 ⅝ x 7 ⅝ in.
Gift of Herbert Waide Hemphill Jr.
in the name of Neal Adair Prince, 1964.1.2

U A **unicorn** is an imaginary horselike creature with magical qualities and a single horn in the middle of its forehead. Unicorns, which are wild and seldom caught, appear often in medieval poems, stories, and paintings. Edgar Tolson, the artist who made this carving, lived in the mountains of Kentucky. He began carving toys when he was eight years old. He went on to become a farmer and later, a preacher. When he reached his early fifties, he resumed **"whittling"** animals out of poplar wood with a small pocketknife.

Tolson copied this unicorn from a **"tapestry"** (large embroidery) he saw on a postcard, but his unicorn seems more like a pet than a wild creature. He made the fence out of Popsicle sticks. The unicorn's chain was whittled from a single piece of wood, involving a clever technique that uses no cuts or links or glue. In the course of his lifetime, Tolson carved at least **1,000** small figures.

(*What kind of* **personality** *does this unicorn have? What* **color** *would you paint it?*)

Unicorn in a Garden, *c.1972*
Edgar Tolson
Campton, Kentucky
Poplar with Popsicle sticks, cedar, glue, pencil,
leather, and nails, 13 x 11 x 14 in.
Gift of Pat O'Brien Parsons, 1996.12.1

**Figures and Construction
with Blue Border,** *c.1941*
Bill Traylor
Montgomery, Alabama
*Poster paint and pencil on
cardboard, 15 ½ x 8 in.
Gift of Charles and
Eugenia Shannon, 1991.34.1*

V Hold on to your hat! That looks like a high-flying **vulture** just waiting to swoop and scoop goodies from the ground. Bill Traylor used this picture to tell a story. He called these stacked images "**exciting events,**" and you can follow along by starting at the bottom and working your way up. ▶ The dog has chased a cat to the top of a roof—*or is it a tree?*—creating havoc in the neighborhood. ▶ The vulture shows how high in the sky the cat has climbed. ▶ The man is trying to coax the cat to come down. *What do you think will happen if he succeeds?* ▶ You can see excitement in the waving arms and wide-open eyes of the neighborhood people. ▶ One figure is swinging from a tree limb. ▶ Another is running away. *What do you think will happen* **next?**

(*What makes the* **house** *look like a* **tree?**)

The lambs with wolves shall graze the verd
ant mead
And boys in flow'ry bands the tyger lead;
The steer the lion at one crib shall meet,
And harmless serpents lick the pilgrim's feet;
The smiling infant in his hand shall take
The crested basilisk and speckled snake,
Pleas'd, the green lustre of their scales survey,
And with their forky tongues shall *innocently play*

WThe **wolf** on the left is living peacefully with lambs—its prey. The verse in the center predicts that **peace on earth** will occur when wolves and lambs live in harmony. The theme of peace is continued in the flowers, trees, and quiet, grazing animals in the picture. Betsy Lewis drew this sketch in 1801, when she was fifteen years old. Back then, students learned to write and spell by copying verses and illustrating them.

The **wild boar** below is a short-tempered cousin of the farmyard pig. Wild boars live in thick forests to hide from predators. Artist Mike Rodriguez carved this boar from cottonwood. The rough, knotty texture of the log, the jagged edges of the boar's ears, the short horsehair bristles along his spine, and his sharp tusks emphasize his rugged, independent nature.

Page from a Sketchbook:
The Lambs with Wolves, *1801*
Betsy Lewis
Dorchester, Massachusetts
Ink and watercolor on paper, 7 ½ x 6 ¼ in.
Gift of Ralph Esmerian, 1993.10.5

Wild Boar, *1984*
Mike Rodriguez
Rowe Mesa, New Mexico
Paint on cottonwood with horsehair,
marbles, and leather, 11 ½ x 26 ½ x 7 ½ in.
Gift of Elizabeth Wecter, 1985.20.29

X

We often use **"X"** to mean something that is unknown—like the X rays that can illuminate your insides. The creator of this unidentified animal called it a "beast." Miles Carpenter, an artist from Virginia, ran a sawmill; when business was slow, he started carving small animals to pass the time. He would sometimes look at pieces of rough wood and see the shapes of animals, calling them **"root monsters."** The natural twists, curves, and bumps influenced the form of his sculptures. *Does this unidentified creature seem fierce or friendly?*

(What name would *you* give it?)

Beast, *late 20th century*
Miles Burkholder Carpenter
Waverly, Virginia
Paint on wood with rubber ears,
26 x 39 ½ x 33 in.
Blanchard-Hill Collection, gift of M. Anne Hill
and Edward V. Blanchard Jr., 1998.10.14

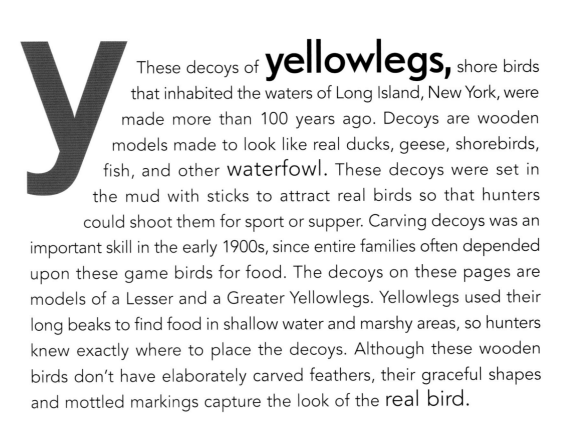

y These decoys of **yellowlegs,** shore birds that inhabited the waters of Long Island, New York, were made more than 100 years ago. Decoys are wooden models made to look like real ducks, geese, shorebirds, fish, and other **waterfowl.** These decoys were set in the mud with sticks to attract real birds so that hunters could shoot them for sport or supper. Carving decoys was an important skill in the early 1900s, since entire families often depended upon these game birds for food. The decoys on these pages are models of a Lesser and a Greater Yellowlegs. Yellowlegs used their long beaks to find food in shallow water and marshy areas, so hunters knew exactly where to place the decoys. Although these wooden birds don't have elaborately carved feathers, their graceful shapes and mottled markings capture the look of the **real bird.**

(*What other animals have* **long legs?**)

Greater Yellowlegs, *c. 1910*
Artist unidentified
Eastern United States
Paint on wood, 14 ½ x 2 ⅞ x 4 in.
Gift of Alistair B. Martin, 1969.1.122

Lesser Yellowlegs, *c. 1900*
Probably Verity family member
Long Island, New York
Paint on wood and canvas, 10 ⅜ x 4 ½ x 1 ½ in.
Gift of Cordelia Hamilton, 1963.4.3

Z Can you find a **zebra** in this map of animals? Here is a hint: Zebras live in Africa. This map of carefully drawn animals and different people in native dress was probably made by a schoolgirl in New England in 1835. Students learned geography as a basic introduction to history, biography, and travel—knowing where all the animals lived was an essential part of education. Female students often created maps using **❝needlepoint❞** (yarn stitched onto canvas) or **❝embroidery❞** (colored thread stitched onto silk or linen cloth). This schoolgirl map is unusual because it was drawn with pencil and ink and painted with a wash of very thin watercolors.

(*Now that our travels through the alphabet are complete, find a home for all the critters in this book on the map!*)

Map of the Animal Kingdom, *1835*
Artist unidentified
Probably New England
Watercolor, ink, and pencil on paper, 26 x 34¾ in.
Promised gift of Ralph Esmerian, P1.2001.269

Special thanks go to Gerard C. Wertkin, director, and Tanya Heinrich, exhibition
catalog and book editor, and their colleagues at the American Folk Art Museum:
Brooke Davis Anderson, director and curator of The Contemporary Center;
Sue Conlon, assistant to the director; Marie S. DiManno, director of museum shops;
Janey Fire, director of photographic services; Rosemary Gabriel, director
of publications; Evelyn R. Gurney, book buyer; Rebecca Hayes, manager of school
and docent programs; Stacy C. Hollander, senior curator and director of
exhibitions; Lee Kogan, director of the Folk Art Institute and curator of special
projects for The Contemporary Center; Ann-Marie Reilly, chief registrar and
director of exhibition production; Celene Ryan, curatorial assistant;
Diana Schlesinger, director of education; and Judith Gluck Steinberg, director
of traveling exhibitions. Additional thanks go to Benjamin J. Boyington.